WORKBOOK

The Healing Marriage

Principles and prayers
for flourishing couples

Daniel and Esther Baumgartner

Bethesda Heilungsdienst
healing encounters & resources

Title: The Healing Marriage Workbook: Principles and prayers for flourishing couples
Copyright © 2024 Daniel Baumgartner & Esther Baumgartner.

Print: ISBN 978-3-9525900-6-5

Published by: Verein Bethesda Heilungsdienst, Zurich
info@bethesda-heilungsdienst.ch
www.bethesda-heilungsdienst.ch

Editorial & design: Bright Books, Kyiv, Ukraine, bspub@me.com
Illustrations: Claudia Huber, claudiahuber-illustration.de

Scriptures are taken from the Holy Bible, New International Version®, NIV®. Copyright © 1973, 1978, 1984, 2011 by Biblica, Inc.™ Used by permission of Zondervan. All rights reserved worldwide. www.zondervan.com. The "NIV" and "New International Version" are trademarks registered in the United States Patent and Trademark Office by Biblica, Inc.™

Disclaimer: This is a companion workbook to the "The Healing Marriage: Principles and prayers for flourishing couples" book and is not designed as a stand-alone publication. This is a self-help workbook with advice on marriage and relationships. It assumes a spiritual worldview that is consistent with the teachings of the New Testament. Prayer for deliverance has been practiced by followers of Christ throughout history. It has always been a controversial topic. Readers must exercise discernment in the way they apply the contents of this book and are responsible for adapting the material to their individual situation and marriage. The authors and Verein Bethesda Heilungsdienst disclaim all responsibility for any loss, damage, or disruption due to errors or omissions in the information and advice given in this book, whether such errors or omissions result from negligence, accident, or any other cause. The authors insist on the importance of accurately discerning the difference between spiritual, emotional, and physical issues and explicitly advise readers to take into account the advice of relevant specialists, including physicians, psychologists, or marriage counsellors.

Welcome to The Healing Marriage Workbook!

This workbook is designed to help you better understand, and apply, the approach and prayers at the heart of *The Healing Marriage* book. You will find questions, exercises or worksheets to go with each chapter of the book. Whether studying on your own, with your spouse or in a group, this valuable resource will help you organise your thoughts, learning and journal your experiences as you start to use the prayer tools or implement practical change. It is a resource you will want to keep coming back to again and again as you continue to grow your relationship.

 Finding your way around

Basic Study

You will find Pause for thought, Questions on and Prayers sections at the end or within most chapters in the book. These have been reproduced here, chapter by chapter, but this time we've included space for you to write your answers, notes etc. directly below each question or exercise.

Further Study

The Further study questions included for each chapter are a chance for you to dive even deeper into some of the topics touched on in the chapters.

Worksheets

We've included photocopiable worksheets for some chapters. Use these to help you identify and work on key emotional, spiritual or practical issues in a structured way.

Making the most of your study

1. Pray before starting your study and invite the Holy Spirit to guide and speak to you.
   Be determined to work on any issues he shows you that need addressing.
2. Read the relevant chapter in *The Healing Marriage* book, if you haven't already done so. Then answer the questions, do the exercises or pray the suggested prayers.
3. The Holy Spirit may draw you into deeper times of study, reflection and prayer around certain topics, so be open to his leading. Mark the things you want to come back to later.
4. Keep the book and workbook handy for reference in everyday life. So for example, open the book at the relevant prayer steps/ prayer tools when you pray for each other.
5. When you make progress in one area, go back over the material to identify the next area you want to focus on together.

<table>
<tr><td>

The Healing Marriage approach is about:
- Discerning spiritual and emotional roots of issues spoiling your love
- Using the 5 healing and freedom prayer tools to deal with these roots effectively
- Taking practical steps to promote peace and walk in unity
- Learning new skills to grow your relationship

</td><td>

This study material will help you:
- Grow closer together and be more united
- Communicate better and reduce tension
- Deal with the sin spoiling your relationship
- Heal emotional hurts making change difficult
- Discern spiritual attack and pray for deliverance

</td></tr>
</table>

CONTENTS

Introduction 5

Chapter 1: One heart and one soul 7
Chapter 2: The power of the marriage covenant 8
Chapter 3: A new creation 9
Chapter 4: Identifying obstacles to unity 11
Chapter 5: Overcoming obstacles to unity 13
Chapter 6: Tips for growing in unity 14
Chapter 7: Laying the right foundations 15
Chapter 8: Prioritising Communication 16
Chapter 9: Overcoming our differences 17
Chapter 10: Communication killers 18
Chapter 11: From battlefields to radio silence 19
Chapter 12: Communication and conflict resolution 20
Chapter 13: Nowhere to hide 21
Chapter 14: Recognising sin in marriage 22
Chapter 15: Overcoming sin in marriage 23
Chapter 16: Prayer tool for restoration 25
Chapter 17: Hitting the target 27
Chapter 18: The power of healing in marriage 28
Chapter 19: Breaking negative patterns of hurt 29
Chapter 20: Healing past and present wounds 30
Chapter 21: Dealing with negative reactions 31
Chapter 22: When memories torment us 32
Chapter 23: The power of deliverance in marriage 33
Chapter 24: The spiritual realm around us 34
Chapter 25: Identifying and closing entry points 35
Chapter 26: Praying for deliverance in marriage 36
Chapter 27: Getting better results 37

Worksheets 39
   How united are we? 40
   Share meals 41
   Plan a date 42
   Do things together 43
   Work on common projects 44
   Look for the treasure 45
   Take a walk down memory lane 46
   Creating your unique marriage culture 47
   Tip 1: Don't give up! 48
   Tip 2: Set aside time 49
   Tip 3: Identify bitter roots 50
   Tip 4: Forgive each other 50
   Tip 5: Schedule business meetings 51
   Talking about sex 54

Contact and online information 55

The Healing Marriage approach

1. The Healing Marriage approach is simple: As couples learn to pray for each other in the key areas of forgiveness, healing and deliverance, things that may not be going so well in their relationship can actually start to get better!

a. In what ways could praying for each other benefit your marital relationship?

b. How familiar are you with the idea of ministering to each other in the areas of forgiveness, healing and deliverance?

2. In 2 Corinthians 5:17 it says:

"Therefore, if anyone is in Christ, the new creation has come: The old has gone, the new is here!"

a. In what areas of your marriage would you say "the new" has come?

b. Are there any areas where "the old" is still present?

c. How would you explain the paradox that, although we are a new creation in Christ, we can still struggle with "the old"?

3. It takes determination and effort to build a satisfying and happy marriage. How does Philippians 2:12-13 encourage you in this?

"Therefore, my dear friends...continue to work out your salvation with fear and trembling, for it is God who works in you to will and to act in order to fulfil his good purpose."

a. What is your part?

b. What does God do?

c. What is the end result?

4. What challenges have you overcome in your relationship so far? What tools, people, resources etc. did you find most helpful at the time?

🖊️ Setting your study goals

What do you hope to get out of studying *The Healing Marriage* book?
My goals:

1. ....

....

....

2. ....

....

....

3. ....

....

....

What do you hope to get out of the study as a couple?
Our goals:

1. ....

....

....

2. ....

....

....

3. ....

....

....

 Prayer

"Lord, thank you for the gift of marriage. We commit this study to you. Open our hearts and understanding to all you have for us. Give us determination to work on our goals and refresh and renew our love for you and for each other. In Jesus' Name, Amen."

CHAPTER 1:
ONE HEART AND ONE SOUL

▌▌ Pause for thought

1. What does unity in marriage mean to you?

2. In what areas are you already connected and united?

3. What difference might greater unity make to your marriage?

✏️ Further study

1. Do you think that personal growth and development, so highly valued by many people today, is compatible with deeper unity in marriage? Why/ Why not?

2. Think back to the early days of your life together: How did you meet? What attracted you to each other? What made you decide to get married? What were your hopes and dreams for your life together? Write or draw your answers here:

CHAPTER 2: THE POWER OF THE MARRIAGE COVENANT

❙❙ Pause for thought

1. What difference does it make to you to know that your marriage is based on a sacred covenant?

2. Where have you been selfish in your marriage?

If you need to ask your partner's forgiveness say: *"My dearest* .... *(name). I am sorry that I have often put myself first and been selfish. Please forgive me!"*

3. Read Philippians 2:5-11 in your Bible. How can you show love and serve (help, support, bless) your partner, following the example of Jesus in this passage?

I will show love to my partner by (doing, saying, etc.): ....

I plan to do this (date): ....

I will serve my partner by (doing, saying, etc.): ....

I plan to do this (date): ....

🖊 Further study

1. Fill in the gaps in the following description of marriage found in this chapter.

A marriage is a sacred .... between a .... a .... and .... himself. It is a binding .... or agreement which defines .... and commitments.

2. List the privileges and responsibilities of the marriage covenant? (see Ecclesiastes 4:12 and 2 Timothy 2:13):

Privileges	**Responsibilities**

3. In what ways does selfishness undermine the unity between a husband and wife?

CHAPTER 3:
A NEW CREATION

✒ Questions on Relationships with parents

Leaving our parents on a variety of levels is necessary if we want to experience deeper oneness as a couple.

1. Do you feel emotionally free in relation to your parents?

2. Is your partner free in relation to his or her parents?

3. What hinders you from leaving your parents emotionally, spiritually or physically?

🙏 Prayers

Use the prayer from this chapter to pray for freedom in relationship to your parents. Record (in words or pictures) what you experience during prayer (e.g. a pressure in body, headache, sense of relief, lightness etc.).

How do you feel when you think about your parents now?

✏ Further study

Discuss together how you could show love and respect to your parents and parents-in-law whilst at the same time setting healthy boundaries to strengthen your unity as a couple. Jot down notes and any strategies here:

✏️ Questions on freedom from previous sexual partners

Note: This question is personal. It is not always appropriate to share details of previous sexual partners with your spouse. Be sensitive and avoid causing unnecessary pain.

Do you feel free from any previous sexual partners?

🙏 Prayers

Use the prayer from this chapter to pray for freedom from any previous sexual partners. Record (in words or pictures) what you experience during prayer (e.g. a pressure in body, headache, sense of relief, lightness etc.). How do you feel about the person(s) now? How do you feel about the person(s) now?

✏️ Further study

1. Are there any other steps you might need to take to get totally free in this area (e.g. get rid of photos, gifts, re-think practical interaction or arrangements with previous partners where kids are involved, have healing of hurts etc.)?

2. Changing sexual partners or having extra-marital affairs are considered normal in some cultures and circles. Look up 1 Corinthians 6:12-20 in your Bible. How does this passage of Scripture challenge such thinking and help us to remain sexually pure and faithful to each other?

CHAPTER 4: IDENTIFYING OBSTACLES TO UNITY

✏️ Questions on Language and cultural backgrounds

1. List your respective linguistic and cultural backgrounds:

a. My first language and culture:

b. My partner's first language and culture:

2. If you come from different cultural and linguistic backgrounds:

a. How do your differences enrich your relationship?

b. In what ways have you found your differences make it harder to be united?

✏️ Questions on lying

1. Do you find it hard to tell the truth? If so, why and when?

2. Do you come from a family where lying was/is a problem?

🙏 Prayers

Use the 5 prayer steps in this chapter to get free from lying. Record (in word or pictures) anything you experienced during prayer here:

✎ Questions on Negative patterns

1. Is there a negative behaviour pattern in your marriage?

2. Do the same situations lead to the same arguments? If so, when did this negative pattern start? Has it been there since the beginning of your marriage or is it triggered by certain words, looks, situations or memories? Make notes and look for patterns here:

Negative pattern	Triggered by	First started

🙏 Prayers

Talk to God about your observations. Thank him, that he wants to help you to break this negative pattern in your marriage.

CHAPTER 5: OVERCOMING OBSTACLES TO UNITY

✏ Questions on understanding triggers & generational issues

1. In this chapter Daniel shared an example of how he was angry with Esther one day for no reason! The Holy Spirit showed him that his anger was related to negative experiences with a teacher at school. Describe a situation where you reacted badly to your partner, but were not sure why:

2. Can you identify any negative traits, sins or issues that run in your family lines?

Negative trait, sin, issue	Ancestors/family members affected

3. Are any of these present in your life? If so, how are they affecting your marital relationship?

Trait, sin, issue	How it affects us

🙏 Prayers

Use the prayer from the 5 prayer steps in this chapter to get free from generational issues. Record anything you experience as you pray here:

▶ Moving forward: If a spirit has gone, you should experience a change in your thoughts, reactions, behaviour etc. Observe yourself closely over the next days/weeks. Note any changes here:

CHAPTER 6: TIPS FOR GROWING IN UNITY

Questions on tips for growing in unity

1. Why do practical solutions often go hand in hand with healing and freedom prayers?

2. What have you learned in this section on unity?

Further study

1. Review the 6 practical tips for growing in unity suggested in this chapter and choose 1or 2 tips you can start working on now. Jot down your notes and ideas in the table below.

Tip we want to focus on to grow in unity (tick)	Notes
Share meals	
Plan a date	
Do things together	
Work on common projects	
Look for treasure	
Walk down memory lane	

2. Use the worksheets at the back of this workbook to help you get started and keep growing!

CHAPTER 7: LAYING THE RIGHT FOUNDATIONS

⏸ Pause for thought

1. Have you ever had a communication mishap in your marriage?

2. Where do you communicate well with each other?

3. Where could you improve your communication?

✏ Further study

Review the list of Bible verses on talking and listening in this chapter. Which one speaks to you most? Write it out here and learn it by heart.

My memory verse:

CHAPTER 8: PRIORITISING COMMUNICATION

⏸ Pause for thought

1. How easy is it for you to find out how your husband or wife is doing and what they are feeling?

2. How might influences from your upbringing be affecting communication in your marriage today?

3. What kind of communication culture would you like to see in your marriage?

✏ Further study

1. Mark the following statements as True or False and correct them where necessary.

    a. The New Testament was written in Hebrew: T / F
    b. The enemy of our souls is called diabolos in Greek: T / F
    c. Diabolos means 'to encourage', 'to unite' or 'to clarify':   T / F
    d. Speaking kindly to each other strengthens our relationship: T / F

2. In this chapter we mentioned the example of a man who decided to create a different culture of communication in his home from the one he had experienced growing up. Describe or draw the kind of communication culture you experienced in your family of origin. What was positive? What was challenging?

CHAPTER 9: OVERCOMING OUR DIFFERENCES

⏸ Pause for thought

1. Are there any language barriers in your relationship?

2. Do you face any cultural challenges in your marriage?

3. What unique culture would you like to see in your marriage? What steps could you take together to build it?

✏ Further study

1. Use the worksheet, "Creating your unique marriage culture" for more help in this area.

2. Fill in the gaps in the speech bubble below using the following words: details / check / clearly / again.

CHAPTER 10: COMMUNICATION KILLERS

⏸ Pause for thought

Reflect on your communication as a couple:

1. What kind of words do you use with each other?

2. Do you often end up raising your voice?

3. What do you think your face says to your partner?

4. Do you tend to nag or complain a lot at home?

✏ Further study

1. Our words are powerful! Proverbs 18:21 says, *"The tongue has the power of life and death, and those who love it will eat its fruit."* Describe a situation where your words (tongue) brought life or death to your partner?

2. Take a good look at yourself in the mirror. Notice your facial expression. Do you have a bright and friendly face or rather a hard look or appearance?

3. 1 Thessalonians 5:16-18, says, *"Rejoice always, pray continually, give thanks in all circumstances; for this is God's will for you in Christ Jesus."* What can you do instead of nagging and complaining?

CHAPTER 11: FROM BATTLEFIELDS TO RADIO SILENCE

⏸ Pause for thought

1. Have you ever given your spouse the silent treatment?

2. Are you guilty of trying to punish, control or manipulate your partner by what you say or how you say it?

3. Do you need healing or freedom from past experiences negatively affecting your communication as a couple?

✏ Further study

1. What other ways, besides talking, are there to communicate with each other?

2. Proverbs 12:18 says, *"The words of the reckless pierce like swords, but the tongue of the wise brings healing."*

a. What is one of the signs of a reckless person mentioned here?

b. What is one of the fruits of the words of the wise person?

c. Are there situations where it is wiser to remain silent than to speak?

3. In 2 Corinthians 3:17 we read: *"Now the Lord is the Spirit, and where the Spirit of the Lord is, there is freedom"*. How is God's Spirit different from the spirit of domination, control or manipulation?

CHAPTER 12: COMMUNICATION AND CONFLICT RESOLUTION

⏸ Pause for thought

1. What role can you play in building a culture of trust in your marriage?

2. Is there a bitter root poisoning your communication?

3. How could business meetings strengthen your relationship?

4. Is forgetfulness a problem in your marriage? If so, how can you help each other to remember things better?

✏ Further study

Improving your communication and conflict resolution skills in marriage can be challenging, but sometimes a few simple steps in the right direction can make a big difference!

Review the list of 6 tips for improving communication in this chapter, then choose 1 to work on.

Use the worksheets and templates at the end of the workbook to help you get started and make progress.

CHAPTER 13:
NOWHERE TO HIDE

Pause for thought

1. Do you believe that a person can change?

2. Are you willing to face what is inside you? If not, what holds you back (e.g. fear, pride, victim mentality, other…?

3. Do you keep a list (in your head / heart) of the wrong things your partner does? Why / Why not?

Further study

1. Read 1 Corinthians 13: 4-7 and fill in the gaps:

"Love is patient, love is kind. It does not envy, it does not boast, it is not proud. It does not dishonour others, it is not self-seeking, it is not easily angered, it keeps no record of wrongs. Love does not delight in evil but rejoices with the truth. It always protects, always trusts, always hopes, always perseveres."

Fill in the gaps:

"Love is ...., love is .... It does not ...., it does not ...., it is not .... It does not ...., it is not ...., it is not ...., it keeps no .... Love does not ...., but rejoices .... It always ...., always ...., always ...., always ...."

2. Reflect on the above Bible verses. How does your attitude and behaviour towards your partner compare with the biblical standard for love?

3. Exercises to let go of list of wrongs and put on love:

❋ Jot down the things you hold against your partner on a piece of paper. Decide to forgive and let go. As you do so, tear it up and throw away the pieces. Or safely burn the piece of paper.

❋ Hold a heavy stone or book in one hand. Feel the weight and how it tires you. As you speak out forgiveness for each item on your list, pass the book into your other hand. Enjoy the feeling of lightness in your free hand.

CHAPTER 14: RECOGNISING SIN IN MARRIAGE

⏸ Pause for thought

1. What sins might you be tolerating in your life?

2. Can you see any sinful patterns of behaviour in your marriage?

3. Make a decision to stop allowing sin to spoil your life and your marriage!

✏ Further study

1. In Romans 6:23 we read: *"For the wages of sin is death, but the gift of God is eternal life in Christ Jesus our Lord."* How might this verse help you to let go of any sin in your life?

2. Hebrews 12:1-2 says: *"...let us throw off everything that hinders and the sin that so easily entangles. And let us run with perseverance the race marked out for us, fixing our eyes on Jesus, the pioneer and perfecter of faith."*

a. Can you think of an example where you got tangled up in a sin? What helped you to throw it off and get free?

b. How does dealing with sin help us to preserve and run our race?

c. What helps you to keep your eyes fixed on Jesus each day?

CHAPTER 15: OVERCOMING SIN IN MARRIAGE

⏸ Pause for thought

1. Do you admit sins and mistakes, or do you tend to sweep things under the carpet?

2. Can you handle conflict, or do you try to avoid it?

3. Is sin and forgiveness something you can talk about as a couple?

✏ Further study on a foundation for dealing with sin

List the 5 steps for dealing with sin mentioned in this chapter:

1.	4.
2.	5.
3.	

1. Recognise your sin.

a. Read John 16:8,13. Who convicts us of our wrongdoings and shows us truth about ourselves?

b. Read John 8:32. In what way does the truth set us free?

c. Is there anything stopping you from recognising sin in your life (e.g. pride, fear etc.)?

2. Bring your sin to God.

a. According to 1 John 1:9, what does God promise to do when we bring our sin before God?

b. How does this encourage you to let go of any fear or perfectionism?

3. Ask each other's forgiveness.

a. Why is asking each other's forgiveness so important and liberating in marriage?

b. Is there anything stopping you from asking your partner for forgiveness?

4. Be willing to change.

Look up 1 John 2:9-11 in your Bible. In what ways can hatred towards our partner in certain moments blind us to the truth?

5. Commit to truth.

a. What best describes your reaction when confronted with truth about yourself:

defensiveness / anger / withdrawal / blame others / willingness to repent and change / other

b. Talk to God about your reactions. If you don't know why you react as you do, ask him to show you and to help you change where necessary.

c. Why do you think it so important to establish the truth about a given situation before confessing sin or extending forgiveness?

CHAPTER 16: PRAYER TOOL FOR RESTORATION

⏸ Pause for thought

1. Can you accept forgiveness?

2. Can you forgive your partner?

3. Is there anything you need to put right between you? Use the Forgiveness prayers to do so.

🙏 Praying the Forgiveness Prayers

You can say:

1. *"Dear Lord Jesus Christ, I am sorry for* .... *Please forgive me!"*

To partner: *"I am sorry that I have wronged and hurt you with my thoughts, words or actions (be specific). I don't want to do so anymore. Please forgive me!"*

Partner responds: *"I forgive you for what you said or did to me!"*

2. *"Lord Jesus Christ, I accept your forgiveness. Thank you for forgiving me!"*

Where necessary: *"I forgive myself!"*

3. *"Lord Jesus, please show me what I need to put right."*

Record your experience below (in words or pictures):

🖊 Further study

Read The Parable of the Unmerciful Servant in Matthew 18: 23-35.

1. Close your eyes and imagine this story unfolding before you: Where does it take place? What sights or sounds can you see or hear? What happens first? Who says what? What emotions might each person involved experience? What happens next? How does the story end? What feelings does this parable stir up in you?

2. How does this parable help you:

a. Recognise and confess sins (like refusing to forgive) in your life:

b. Ask for and receive God's forgiveness:

c. Forgive others who have wronged you:

CHAPTER 17:
HITTING THE TARGET

⏸ Pause for thought

1. How do you cultivate fellowship with the Lord on a personal level?

2. How do you cultivate fellowship with God as a couple?

✏ Further study

1. What keys to resisting sin can you discover in the following verses:

a. *"I have hidden your word in my heart that I might not sin against you."* (Psalm 119:11)

b. *"So I say, walk by the Spirit, and you will not gratify the desires of the flesh."* (Galatians 5:16)

2. How can you apply these keys to your life on a practical level?

3. How does the following passage from Psalm 51:9-12 help you to cultivate close fellowship with the Lord and each other?

"Hide your face from my sins and blot out all my iniquity. Create in me a pure heart, O God, and renew a steadfast spirit within me. Do not cast me from your presence or take your Holy Spirit from me. Restore to me the joy of your salvation and grant me a willing spirit, to sustain me."

CHAPTER 18: THE POWER OF HEALING IN MARRIAGE

⏸ Pause for thought

1. Have you brought any pain or hurt from your past into your marriage?

2. Do you feel hurt about anything in your marriage today that might need healing?

3. What do you usually do when your spouse or someone else hurts you?

✏ Further study

1. Is anything hindering you from facing up to past or present hurts in your marriage (e.g. wrong teaching, cultural ideas, fear etc.)?

2. Read the powerful prophecy about Jesus the Messiah in Isaiah 53: 3-5:

"He was despised and rejected by mankind, a man of suffering, and familiar with pain. Like one from whom people hide their faces he was despised, and we held him in low esteem. Surely he took up our pain and bore our suffering, yet we considered him punished by God, stricken by him, and afflicted. But he was pierced for our transgressions, he was crushed for our iniquities; the punishment that brought us peace was on him, and by his wounds we are healed."

a. What did Jesus suffer at the hands of men?

b. What did he bear for us?

c. What makes peace possible for us?

d. What brings us healing?

Take a moment to thank Jesus for all he has done on the cross for you!

CHAPTER 19: BREAKING NEGATIVE PATTERNS OF HURT

⏸ Pause for thought

1. Is there a negative pattern of hurt in your marriage?

2. Ask the Holy Spirit to show you what is fuelling it.

3. Together: Ask for forgiveness where you have hurt each other through your words or actions. Ask God to forgive and heal the hurt.

✏ Further study

1. James says: *"Therefore confess your sins to each other and pray for each other so that you may be healed. The prayer of a righteous person is powerful and effective."* (James 5:16)

a. What connection do you see between confessing your sins to each other and praying for healing?

b. Who is considered a righteous person according to the following verse: *"God made him who had no sin to be sin for us, so that in him we might become the righteousness of God."* (2 Corinthians 5:21)

c. What can a righteous person expect to happen when they pray?

CHAPTER 20: HEALING PAST AND PRESENT WOUNDS

❚❚ Pause for thought

1. What inner wound do you want to bring to Jesus?

....

....

2. Do you notice when your partner feels hurt or is not doing so well?

....

....

3. Are you ready to try the Hurts Prayers together?

....

....

🙏 Praying the Hurts Prayers

You can say:

1. "Dear Lord Jesus, I feel hurt because ...."

2. "Lord Jesus, you were hurt by other people. You bore my pain on the cross. This gives you the power to heal my pain. I give my pain to you now. Please heal me!"

3. "I forgive .... (name of person who hurt you) for .... (what he or she said or did to me)!"

Record your experience below (in words or pictures):

CHAPTER 21: DEALING WITH NEGATIVE REACTIONS

⏸ Pause for thought

1. How have your reactions to hurt caused you to hurt yourself or others?

2. Where have you become bitter or said hurtful things?

3. Deal with any wrong reactions using the Reactions Prayers below or in the book.

🙏 Praying the Reactions Prayers

You can say:

1. "Dear Lord Jesus, I feel .... (name your reaction) because of what my partner said or did to me. But I also said or did unkind or unfair things back because I felt hurt."

2. "Lord Jesus, please forgive me for the way I reacted and for holding on to these negative feelings and reactions."

3. "I ask you Lord Jesus to take away these negative feelings of .... I let go of them and give them to you!"

Record your experience below (in words or pictures):

CHAPTER 22: WHEN MEMORIES TORMENT US

⏸ Pause for thought

1. Do you have a painful memory that you would like Jesus to heal?

2. Use the Memories Prayers in the book (or below) to bring this memory to Jesus and invite him to heal you.

✏ Further study

1. Psalm 147:3 says: *"He [God] heals the broken hearted and binds up their wounds."*

a. According to this verse, who heals our broken hearts and binds up the wounds fuelling painful memories?

b. In what way, therefore, is praying for painful memories different to just thinking positively about the past or trying to imagine different endings to certain situations?

🙏 Praying the Memories Prayers

You can say:

1. *"Dear Lord Jesus, please take me back to the painful memory you want to heal!"*

2. *"Please Lord Jesus, come into this painful memory."*

3. *"I forgive .... for what he or she said or did to me. And I ask you Lord Jesus to forgive me for .... (name your reactions to the hurt)."*

Record your experience below (in words of pictures):

CHAPTER 23: THE POWER OF DELIVERANCE IN MARRIAGE

⏸ Pause for thought

1. Do you believe that the unseen or spiritual world can influence your marriage? Why?/Why not?

2. Is there an area of your marriage where you suspect powers of darkness are at work?

✏ Further study

1. How would you describe your current mindset? What influences the way you view the natural and the spiritual world?

2. Romans 12:2 urges us: *"Do not conform to the pattern of this world, but be transformed by the renewing of your mind. Then you will be able to test and approve what God's will is—his good, pleasing and perfect will."*

a. What does it mean to have a renewed mind and why is it so important?

b. How can you take steps to renew your mind in preparation for deliverance?

3. According to the following Bible verses, what has Christ come to do? How do these Scriptures encourage you to seek deliverance?

a. *"The thief [Satan] comes only to steal and kill and destroy; I [Jesus] have come that they may have life, and have it to the full."* (John 10:10)

b. *"He has delivered us from the domain of darkness and transferred us to the kingdom of his beloved Son."* (Colossians 1:13.)

c. *"The reason the Son of God appeared was to destroy the devil's work."* (1 John 3:8b)

CHAPTER 24: THE SPIRITUAL REALM AROUND US

⏸ Pause for thought

1. Thank Jesus that he came to give you abundant life!

2. What is the enemy's strategy to keep you from praying for deliverance? Are there others?

✏ Further study

1. Ephesians 6:12 states: *"For our struggle is not against flesh and blood, but against the rulers, against the authorities, against the powers of this dark world and against the spiritual forces of evil in the heavenly realms."* How does this verse help you to better understand the spiritual dimensions to some of the struggles you face in your marriage?

2. Read Colossians 2:15: *"And having disarmed the powers and authorities, he [Jesus] made a public spectacle of them, triumphing over them by the cross."* Why is it so important for us to understand that Jesus has defeated the powers of darkness?

3. In this chapter, we liken deliverance prayers in everyday life to brushing our teeth. How does this example help you to understand spiritual attack and the role of deliverance in staying spiritually clean and healthy?

CHAPTER 25: IDENTIFYING AND CLOSING ENTRY POINTS

⏸ Pause for thought

1. In what areas of your life do you not feel totally free?

2. How does your lack of freedom affect your marriage?

✎ Further study

1. What are the 3 main entry points for demons mentioned in this chapter? List each one and summarise key teaching:

2. How does understanding how demons gain access to our lives help us prepare for deliverance?

3. What is one of the signs that we are under spiritual attack and may need deliverance?

CHAPTER 26: PRAYING FOR DELIVERANCE IN MARRIAGE

✎ Questions on praying for deliverance

1. Colossians 3:3 says: *"For you died, and your life is now hidden with Christ in God."* How does this truth about your status and identity in Christ give you confidence to pray for deliverance?

2. Read the following Scriptures and complete the sentences:

a. *"When Jesus had called the Twelve together, he gave them power and authority to drive out all demons and to cure diseases, and he sent them out to proclaim the kingdom of God and to heal the sick."* (Luke 9:1-2). Jesus gave the Twelve (his disciples) power and authority to:

b. *"And these signs will accompany those who believe: In my name they will drive out demons"* (Mark 16:17a). This sign will follow those who believe:

c. *"Submit yourselves, then, to God. Resist the devil, and he will flee from you"* (James 4:7). The devil will flee from me if I:

🙏 Praying the Deliverance Prayers

You can say:

1. *"Dear Lord Jesus, I want to be free from* .... *(e.g. bitterness, lust)".*

2. *If someone has sinned against you: "I forgive* .... *(name of person) for* .... *(what he or she did to me)".*

Or: *If you have sinned: "Please Jesus, forgive me for* .... *(what I did, said or thought)".*

3. *"I command the spirit of* .... *(name it according to what it is doing in your life, e.g. fear, hatred) to leave me in the name of Jesus Christ!"*

Record your experience below (in words or pictures):

CHAPTER 27: GETTING BETTER RESULTS

🖊 Questions on combining the prayer tools & staying free

1. List the 5 healing and deliverance prayer tools you can use to pray for transformation in your life and marriage:

2. We often need to use more than one prayer tool to deal with an issue properly. Why do you think that is?

3. What other spiritual resources will help you to walk in healing and freedom (e.g. daily Bible reading, worship, attending church)?

✏ Further study

Consider the following situations. In each case, underline the tool, or tools, you could use to help your partner (or yourself) deal with the spiritual aspects of each one. Discuss your answers:

a. Sadness related to the death of a beloved friend or relative

Hurts Prayer / Reactions Prayers / Memories Prayers / Forgiveness Prayers / Deliverance Prayers

b. Aggressive behaviour after a recent interaction with an ex-partner

Hurts Prayer / Reactions Prayers / Memories Prayers / Forgiveness Prayers / Deliverance Prayers

c. Loss of confidence related to a painful incident (memory)

Hurts Prayer / Reactions Prayers / Memories Prayers / Forgiveness Prayers / Deliverance Prayers

d. Upset in relation to the manipulative behaviour of a sibling or a parent

Hurts Prayer / Reactions Prayers / Memories Prayers / Forgiveness Prayers / Deliverance Prayers

e. Recurring nightmares after witnessing a road accident

Hurts Prayer / Reactions Prayers / Memories Prayers / Forgiveness Prayers / Deliverance Prayers

f. Guilt related to sinful habit that is difficult to kick

Hurts Prayer / Reactions Prayers / Memories Prayers / Forgiveness Prayers / Deliverance Prayers

Worksheets

How united are we?

1. Marital satisfaction has much to do with the ability to grow in unity together. How would you rate your overall unity as a couple?

Very united / fairly united / fairly disunited / very disunited / not sure

2. On a scale of 1-5, with 1 being very disunited and 5 being very united, how would you rate your unity in each of the following areas? Use the space on the right to add comments & observations:

Areas	Rate	Comments
Spiritual beliefs, values and goals		
Goals to work towards		
Sexual satisfaction		
Relationship to work		
Money and how to spend it		
Practical parenting		
Relationship to extended family		
Use of our free time		
Value placed on friendships		
Organisation of household		
Other...		

3. Choose 1 area to work on. In your opinion, where are you united in this area and why? And where are you disunited and why?

Area of focus:	Where we are united:	Where we are disunited and why:

4. Share your answers with each other: What is important to both of you? Where do you tend to disagree or pull in different directions? Where can one or both of you let go (of your idea, way of doing things etc.) or agree to meet each other halfway?

Share meals

1. How often do we share meals together?

2. Are we both happy with our current arrangement? If not, why not?

3. How can we make space for shared meals (e.g. adjust work/family routines, re-order priorities)?

4. How can we make shared meals a highlight we both look forward to in our day or week? Here are a few ideas. Tick the ones you want to try, or add your own ideas to the end of the list:

- ☐ Plan healthy menus using the best quality ingredients you can afford.
- ☐ Cook each other's favourite foods now and again.
- ☐ Ensure environment you eat in is clean and tidy.
- ☐ Set the table properly.
- ☐ Decorate the table with placemats, flowers, candles etc.
- ☐ Focus on reducing any noise and stress with kids, if a problem.
- ☐ Play relaxing background music.
- ☐ Keep mobile phones out of reach and on airplane mode.
- ☐ Think of topics/questions to ask each other to show interest and make the most of the conversation opportunities.
- ☐ Keep things positive. Avoid gossip, negative talk or depressing topics out of your control.
- ☐ Include faith at the table. Give thanks to God for the food and time together before eating.
- ☐ End evening meals with a short time of Bible reading and family prayers.

- ☐ Other ideas...

Plan a date

Brainstorm ideas for stay at home, going out dates and special occasions:

Stay at home date	Going out dates	Special occasions

Date planner template:

When (date, time):

What (stay at home/going out activity):

Preparations (reservations, babysitter, etc. and who will do what):

Outfits and hair (look your best and feel attractive!):

Date evaluation template:

What did you enjoy most (highlight)?

Was anything challenging?

Would you want to do this again? Why/why not?

Do things together

1. What household chores or other tasks could we help each other with?

2. What do you enjoy doing most in your free time? Jot down your individual preferences:

You	Your partner

3. Review your preference lists:

a. What could you do together?

b. What could you do on your own?

c. How could you still show interest and support each other when doing different things?

4. Is there a dream trip, outing or activity you could plan to do in the foreseeable future? Brainstorm ideas here:

Work on common projects

1. Focusing on something beyond ourselves and our needs pleases the Lord and helps us to grow as a couple. Read Galatians 6:9-10 and reflect on the following questions together:

"Let us not become weary in doing good, for at the proper time we will reap a harvest if we do not give up. Therefore, as we have opportunity, let us do good to all people, especially to those who belong to the family of believers."

a.   Is it possible to get tired of helping others?
b.   How does this verse encourage you to keep doing good?
c.   Who should we help?

2. There are endless needs in the world and many ways you can do good as a couple! The key is to serve with the gifts and resources you have and not what you don't have (see 1 Peter 4:10). Review the following list of areas for service, and tick those that resonate with you, or add your own ideas:

▶   Helping others:

▶   Contributing to church life:

▶   Getting involved in neighbourhood projects:

▶   Supporting charities:

▶   Playing on a local sports team:

▶   Other…

Pray about the possibilities and ideas you discussed together. Ask God to guide you and show you how he wants to use you as a couple to do good and bless others. Write down any thoughts, pictures, verses etc. that come to you as you pray:

Look for the treasure

Reminding ourselves of all the good things in our marriage keeps us positive and moving in the right direction! Write or draw a list of your partner's good qualities:

▶ What is he or she particularly good at?

▶ What do you like most about him or her?

▶ How does he or she make your life better?

▶ What are you thankful for?

▶ Etc.

Take a walk down memory lane

1. Travel back in time to your early days together: How you met and fell in love, what attracted you to each other, your courtship, wedding and the early days of your marriage and on through the years until now. Jot down memories and thoughts in the different boxes.

How did we meet? And what made
me fall in love with my husband/wife?

What was it about him/her that
I admired or was attracted to?

What are some of my favourite
memories from our time together so far?

What are our special songs, places
to hang out or visit, favourite photos etc.

2. Share your answers and memories with each other. Take time to celebrate how you found each other and the fact that you still have each other today! Try looking into each other's eyes and saying: "You are still the love of my life!"

Creating your unique marriage culture

When we get married, God creates something new. This includes the opportunity to create a unique culture within our marriage, one based on clear biblical values and principles, while drawing on the best of what each of us brings to the marriage from our respective backgrounds.

1. What spiritual, cultural or linguistic components do you each bring to your marriage (e.g. set of values, spiritual practices, social norms, family traditions, language spoken etc.)?

You	Your partner

2. Pick one and reflect on the following questions: Does this contradict biblical teaching? How important is it to you? In what ways does it enrich your relationship today? In what ways might this be fuelling tension and division? How do you see it fitting into the unique marriage culture you want to create together?

3. Share your answers with each other and try to reach a conclusion: What positive aspects can you incorporate into your new marriage culture? What negative elements can you discard? When you have reached a decision that you are both comfortable with, record it here:

▶ Area of focus:

▶ Decision reached:

▶ Action required:

Tip 1: Don't give up!

Power Decisions & Prayers

Improving communication in marriage starts with a decision. Decide today that you want to learn to communicate better with your spouse! Fill out, sign and date the power decisions below. Pin them up at home or place them in your Bible to remind yourself of your goals.

Power Decision: Yes to good communication!

"I want to communicate better with my partner. With this goal in mind, I will work to improve my communication skills, step by step. I will start by focusing on ....

....

....

....

....

....

.... "

Name & Date: ....

Power Decision: Kick out bad communication!

"I choose to stop (shouting, stonewalling, nagging etc.) ....

....

....

....

I no longer want to communicate in this way."

Name & Date: ....

Power Decision: Learn a better way!

"I want to learn to (listen carefully, express my gratitude, speak kind words etc.) ....

....

....

....

....

....

.... "

Name & Date: ....

Power Decision: Ask God to help you!

"Dear Lord Jesus, I want to communicate better with my spouse, but I need your help!! I am sorry where I have communicated badly, particularly for (name negative communication) ....

....

Please forgive me! Help me to learn to ....

....

(name better way). In Jesus' Name, Amen."

Tip 2: Set aside time

1. How easy do you find it to create space in your schedule for good communication?

Easy / quite easy / quite hard / very hard

2. How could you create more opportunities for communication (e.g. plan date nights, shared meals, common projects, stop certain current activities to make time etc.). Discuss together and make notes here:

3. Sharing feelings, fears and dreams takes communication to a whole new level. These questions will help you to get going. Can you think of others?

▶ What are you both enjoying at the moment?

▶ What do you find difficult?

▶ What are your hopes and dreams for the future?

▶ What are your fears for the future?

4. How could you show interest and empathy even if you don't fully understand your partner's feelings or what they're going through?

5. Why do you think that perfectionism or performance-orientated mindsets keep us from connecting at a deeper level?

Tip 3: Identify bitter roots

1. Is there a particular topic that you no longer want to talk about with your partner? Why do you think this is?

2. Sometimes we can end up feeling bitter towards our partner over certain issues or past situations. We may find it hard to let go or forgive. These feelings can hinder communication between us. But Hebrews 12:15 urges us to deal with bitterness quickly: *"See to it that no one falls short of the grace of God and that no bitter root grows up to cause trouble and defile many."*

a. Do you think there is a connection between falling short of God's grace and bitterness?

b. Why do you think bitterness is described in terms of a root in this verse?

c. In what way can the bitterness in one person cause trouble and defile others around them? Can you think of an example?

3. Ask the Holy Spirit to show you any bitterness in your life hindering your communication. (Then move onto Tip 4: Forgive each other)

Tip 4: Forgive each other

1. Once you have identified any bitter roots, decide, with God's help, to forgive your partner and let go of the resentment.

You can say: *"Dear Lord, I bring the bitterness I feel towards* .... *(person) about* ......
.... *(situation). I decide to let go of it today and to forgive him/her in the Name of Jesus, Amen".*

2. Pause for a moment and observe how you react to this prayer. Can you forgive, or is it a struggle? If you can't forgive, you may need some more healing of hurts and/or deliverance before you can fully forgive. Note down your experiences in prayer here:

Tip 5: Schedule business meetings

Good planning and coordination of tasks reduces tension and potential conflict. Schedule regular 'marriage business meetings' to deal with the practical details of home and family. Use the template "Our Marriage Business Meeting" to help you plan and structure your meetings.

Tips on planning and structuring a marriage business meeting

▶   Set a date and a start and end time for the meeting.

▶   Agree prior to the meeting on 1-3 topics for discussion.

▶   During the meeting, focus on what needs to be done, by whom, and by when.

▶   Write down decisions reached.

▶   Schedule date and topics for next (follow-up) meeting.

▶   Use the "Marriage Business Meeting Template" to structure and record the meeting.

Checklist of possible topics to focus on in a marriage business meeting:

☐   Planning of marriage or date nights.

☐   Planning leisure activities, outings and holidays.

☐   Children or grandchildren's progress, needs and requests.

☐   Needs of aging parents or other relatives.

☐   New purchases.

☐   The cleaning and laundry.

☐   Renovation or repairs to your home.

☐   Gardening and other work around the house.

☐   Car or bike repairs.

☐   Requests from other people to do things.

☐   Meeting with friends.

☐   Church or ministry involvement.

☐   Business related to charities or clubs.

☐   Other...

Useful Templates:

✺ **Our Marriage Business Meeting**

✺ **Reminder Notes**

OUR MARRIAGE BUSINESS MEETING

Date: ....   Topics to be discussed:

Time: ....   1. ....

Place: ....   2. ....

Date next meeting: ....   3. ....

Topic 1:

Conclusion:

Action steps (who will do what & by when):

Topic 2:

Conclusion:

Action steps (who will do what & by when):

Topic 3:

Conclusion:

Action steps (who will do what & by when):

REMINDER NOTES

Jot down key information about upcoming appointments /activities/events on these photocopiable templates. Display in a visible location for stress-free coordination.

HIS Activity:

Preparations:

Logistics:

Notes:

Date & Time:

HER Activity:

Preparations:

Logistics:

Notes:

Date & Time:

OUR Activity:

Preparations:

Logistics:

Notes:

Date & Time:

Talking about sex

Most couples would agree that regular, good sex is important. But what do each of us mean by "good" and how often is "regular"? Talking about sex can be a bit awkward. This is particularly true if either of you have experienced sexual brokenness in the past, or if things aren't going too well at the moment. There can be many reasons why sex can be difficult and talking about it can be even harder. But as we become increasingly healed and free, the quality of our marital relationship will grow, leading to greater sexual satisfaction together.

Tips on talking about sex:

▶ Create a safe space for both of you to communicate emotional and physical needs. Approach any dialogue with sensitivity, love and respect.

▶ Listen patiently to what your partner shares about their needs, wants, desires or fears, as far as they are able to put these into words. Look out for non-verbal signals as well.

▶ Be willing to meet them halfway if they want more or less sex than you would prefer or when it comes to trying new things.

Dialogue questions to get started:

☐ How important is sex to you in a relationship?

☐ How often would you like to have sex (every day, twice a week, once a month etc.)?

☐ How can we reach an agreement on a frequency we both feel comfortable with? (This may involve compromise on both sides)

☐ How can we plan time for sex? (Far from inhibiting passion, many couples find it helpful to purposely plan space for sex)

☐ How can we create an atmosphere where each of us feels safe, relaxed and able to open up? (Settings, lighting, privacy, etc. make a difference)

☐ How do you like to be touched and what gives you the most pleasure?

☐ What positions do you find most enjoyable?

☐ What turns you on? Is anything a "no-go" for you?

☐ How can I initiate sex in a way that would interest you?

☐ What new things could we try or explore together?

☐ Are there situations where we have deliberately deprived each other of sex (as punishment, to get our own way etc.)?

☐ Are there situations were we have agreed to abstain from sex for a time (e.g. difficult pregnancy, times of deeper prayer)?

☐ Etc.....

CONTACT AND ONLINE INFORMATION

Do you need more support?

We believe that any couple who applies the prayers and principles presented in this workbook can experience real change. Some people find it helpful to talk and pray with someone else. You can find out more about our counselling services and resources on our website.

Did you enjoy this study?

Write and tell us how the workbook has helped you. We would love to hear from you!

You can play an important role in helping other couples find healing and freedom by recommending this book to your friends and sharing it on social media.

Many people rely on workbook reviews to help them decide whether or not to buy a workbook. Please consider leaving a short review on the platform where you purchased your copy.

If you ordered from Bethesda Heilungsdienst, you can email your review to us at the address below. Thank you very much!

bethesda-heilungsdienst.ch

info@bethesda-heilungsdienst.ch